From South Korea:

Graphic design from South Korea, compiled and published by Counter-Print

First published in 2021 © Counter-Print
ISBN 978-1-8381865-2-4 Designed by Counter-Print
www.counter-print.co.uk

With special thanks to all the contributors.

South Korea, known as 'The Land of the Morning Calm', is a country of contrasts, where the ultra modern meets the traditional. One of the world's largest economies, its culture has come to be celebrated worldwide.

Officially the Republic of Korea, South Korea is a country in East Asia, constituting the southern part of the Korean Peninsula and sharing a land border with their enigmatic neighbours to the North. It is a country of roughly 25 million people, with around half of its inhabitants living in Seoul.

Its first kingdom was noted in Chinese records in the early 7th century BCE. Following the unification of the Three Kingdoms of Korea in the late 7th century, it was ruled by the Goryeo (918–1392) and the Joseon (1392–1897) dynasties. The succeeding Korean Empire was annexed into the Empire of Japan in 1910. After World War II, Korea was divided into Soviet and American administered zones. In 1950, a North Korean invasion began the Korean War and after its end in 1953, the country's economy began to boom, a period known as the 'Miracle on the Han'.

Since the turn of the 21st century, South Korea has emerged as a major exporter of popular culture, which has become a significant part of its burgeoning economy. The growing popularity of Korean pop culture in the world was at least partly driven by the South Korean government supporting its creative industries through subsidies and funding for start-ups, as a form of soft power with the goal of becoming a leading global exporter of culture. In 2014 alone, the South Korean government allocated 1% of its annual budget to cultural industries and raised a $1 billion fund to nurture popular culture.

South Korea's influential pop culture is a phenomenon referred to as the 'Korean Wave', which since the 1980s, has heavily impacted contemporary culture, music, film and television industries throughout the world; carried by the Internet, social media and the proliferation of K-pop music videos on YouTube. As well as the world-famous K-Pop, K-Beauty and K-Food, the last few years have also seen an explosion in Korean graphic design. Its development is intertwined with the country's complex history, from the invention of the Hangul alphabet in the late Joseon Dynasty, to Japanese occupation, Korean independence, US imperialism and the end of the Korean War.

Design education was established after the War and many teachers of this generation were trained during Japanese rule or in Japan, which created an understanding of graphic design that leant towards a Japanese approach. After Korea gained independence, the government also provided scholarships for students to study design abroad in the United States. When they returned, they introduced a new way of learning from the US and reimagined graphic design curriculum in Korea.

The contemporary Korean design community carries on this legacy, blending many influences seamlessly, with new trends continuously being embraced, while time-old traditions such as the Hangul alphabet are updated at a dizzying speed. The last few years have seen South Korean typography in particular explode, with young type designers and lettering artists, exploring this script.

The Korean alphabet, known as 'Hangul' in South Korea and 'Chosŏn'gŭl' in North Korea, is a writing system for the Korean language created by King Sejong the Great in 1443. The letters for the five basic consonants reflect the shape of the speech organs used to pronounce them, and they are systematically modified to indicate phonetic features. Hangul is considered a core aspect of Korean identity and, as the country's own alphabet, it helps differentiate South Korea from its East Asian neighbours. As seen in the pages of this book, designers today continue to explore the alphabet's possibilities and test its limits in new and exciting ways.

Graphic design in South Korea has been shaped by foreign influences and this cross-pollination of ideas has been accelerated in the age of the internet and social media. But, instead of becoming homogenised, to its credit South Korean design remains fascinating – it is both familiar and innovative and its amalgamation of influences make it unique and unpredictable. Korean design combines complete opposites, uniting them to create a form of design that is simple and bold, modern and traditional, personal and collective, digital and analogue. But to fully understand what sets Korean design apart from all the rest, you have to look at the people behind it.

Jon Dowling
Counter-Print

Studio Fnt

From South Korea

studiofnt.com

Record284 — Culture on a Turntable
Identity for an exhibition exploring music culture
2020

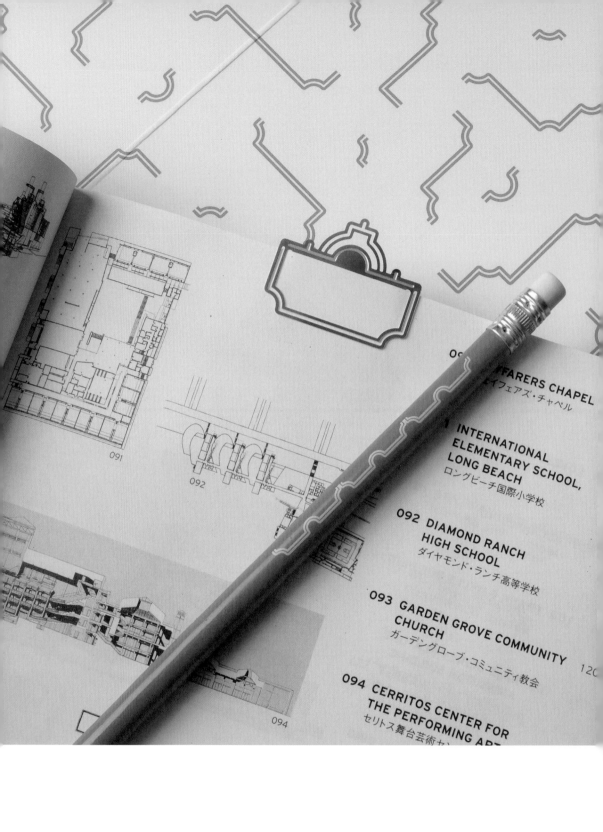

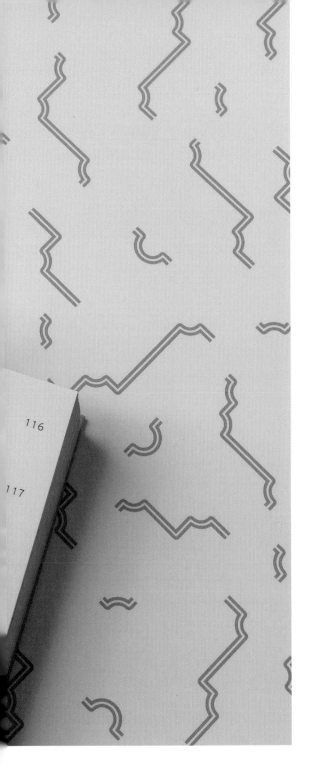

116

117

Culture Station Seoul 284
Branding for a multi-purpose, cultural space
2017

2 대성한지

3 대승한지마을

4 덕치전통한지

5 문경전통한지

6 성일한지

7 신풍한지

8 신현세전통한지

9 안동한지

10 용인한지

11 원주전통한지

12 원주한지

13 이상옥 전통한지

14 장지방

15 전주전통한지원

16 청양파앤비

Daeseung Hanji Maeul

Deokchi Jeontong Hanji

Mungyeong Jeontong Hanji

Seongil Hanji

Sinpung Hanji

Sinhyeonse Jeontong Hanji

Andong Hanji

Yongin Hanji

Wonju Jeontong Hanji

Wonju Hanji

Yeesangok Jeontong Hanji

Jang ji Bang

Cheongyang P&B

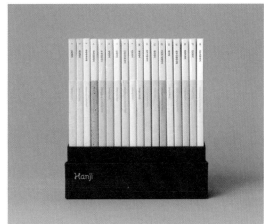

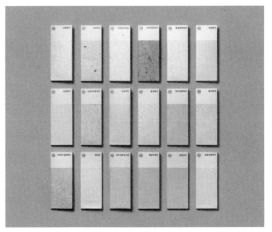

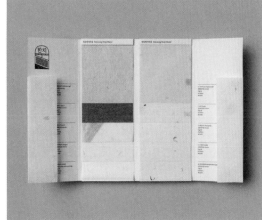

Hanji Sample Book

Sample books for KDCF's (Korea Craft and Design Foundation) Hanji business

2018

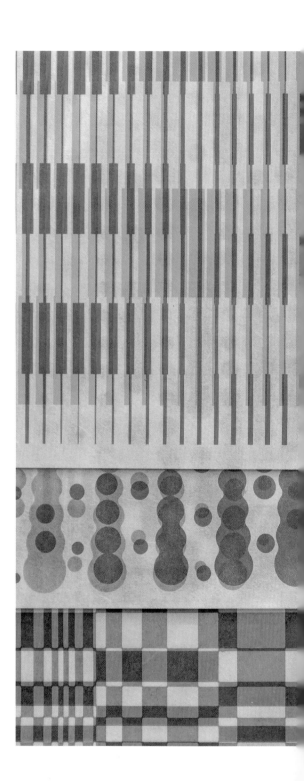

TWL Original Hanji and Products

Design series of Hanji papers for lifestyle
shop TWL
2020

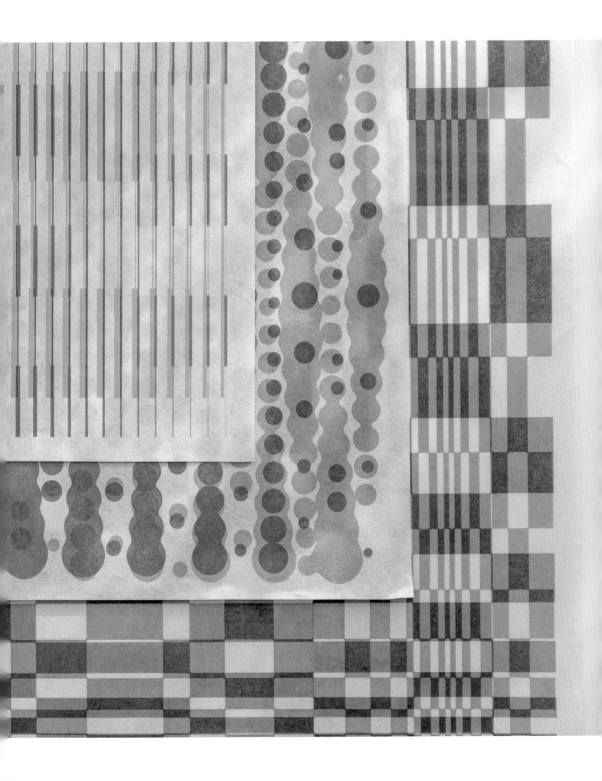

Studio Fnt

National Theater of Korea:

Repertory Season

Identity for an annual
season program
2019–2020

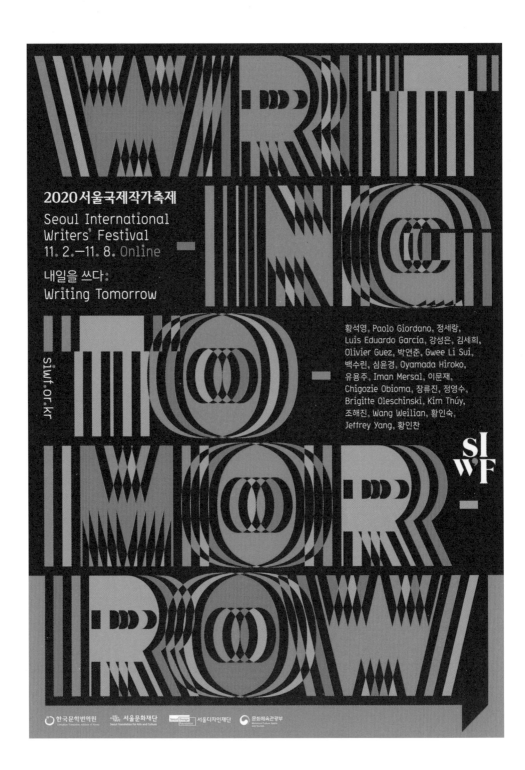

Writing Tomorrow: 2020 Seoul International Writers' Festival

Poster design for a festival

2020

Bohuy Kim

4th Seoul Dance Film Festival. Poster design for Media art Forum. 2020.

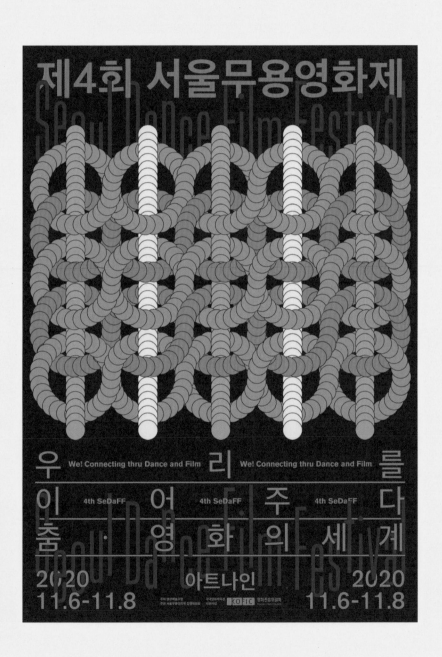

From South Korea

kimbohuy.com

Seoul Peace-Culture Festival

Seoul Peace-Culture Festival

2019 서울평화문화축제
평화의 이야기를 시작하는 작은 움직임
2019. 11. 9. (토) 13:00-19:00
평화문화진지

2019 Seoul Peace-Culture Festival
Talk peace, Begin to move
2019. 11. 9. (Sat) 13:00-19:00
Peace Culture Bunker

주최 도봉문화재단   주관 사장님들   협력 동네형들, 축제행성   후원 서울시, 도봉구

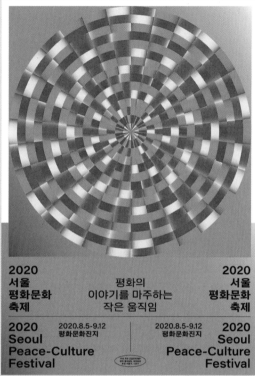

Seoul Peace-Culture Festival

Poster designs for a cultural festival
2019–2020

→

Odd Hyphen 2021

Poster designs for a design studio
2021

ODD-HYPHEN

2021

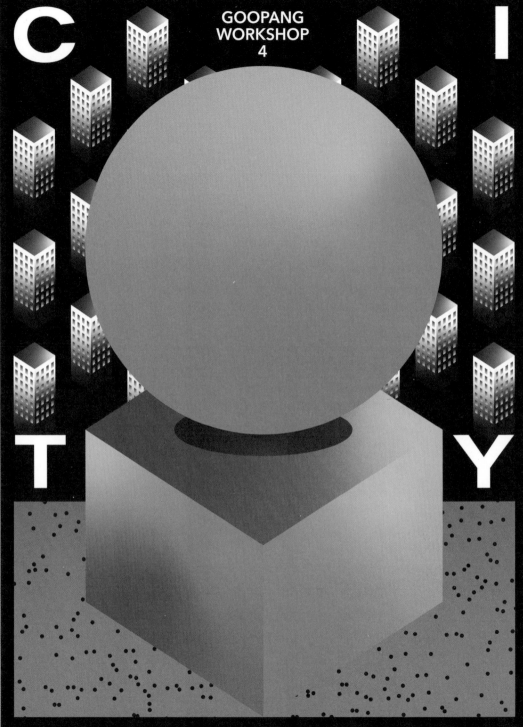

C I

GOOPANG
WORKSHOP
4

T Y

11.28　　　　　SCD 225-8 4F　　　　　11.29

Goopang 4
Poster designs for an art group
2020

→
Park Hyeonmi
Poster design for a dance company
2020

홈트족을 위한 한국춤 활용법

호흡 디딤

2020.10.24 Sat
re-DANCE 한국문화예술위원회

DANCE!
DANCE!
DANCE!
DANCE!

한국문화예술위원회 re-DANCE
2020.10.24 Sat

유튜브 ☞ [Re-Dance] Park hyeonmi

Eunjoo Hong and Hyungjae Kim

Mad Pride Seoul. Event identity for Antica, a cultural organisation for the mentally disabled. 2019.

From South Korea

hongxkim.com

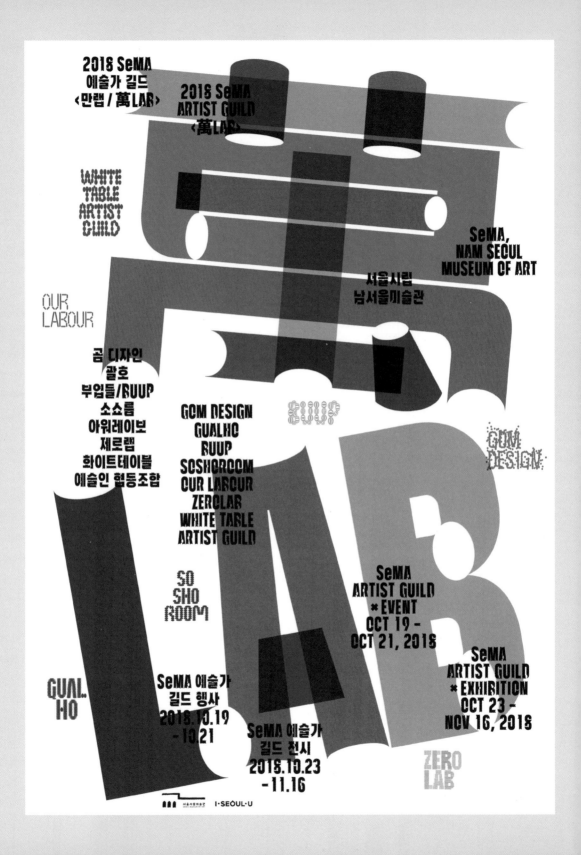

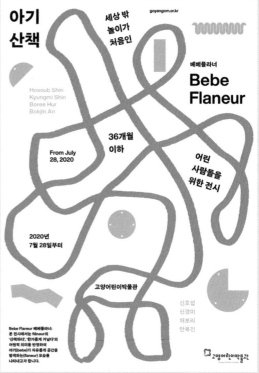

←
2018 SeMA Artist Guild Lab
Poster design for Seoul Museum of Art
2018

Bebe Flaneur
Poster designs for Goyang Children's Museum
2020

Artience Daejeon
Poster design for Daejeon Culture and Arts Foundation
2019

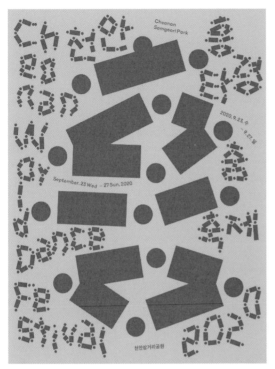

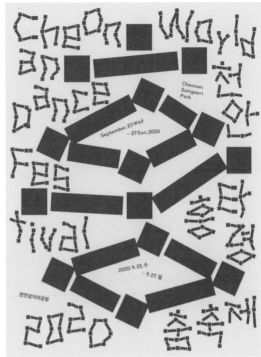

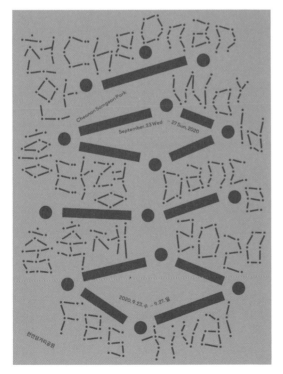

Cheonan World Dance Festival

Identity for a dance festival
2020

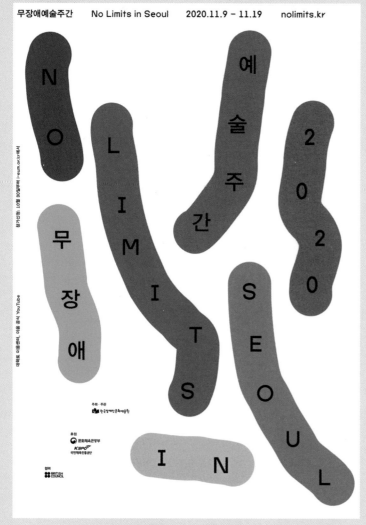

무장애예술주간 No Limits in Seoul 2020.11.9 – 11.19 nolimits.kr

Eunjoo Hong and Hyungjae Kim

No Limits in Seoul
Poster designs for the Korea
Disability Arts & Culture Center
2020

→
play:ground
Poster design for Wooran
Foundation
2019

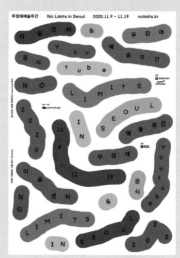

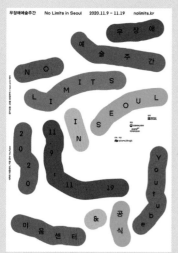

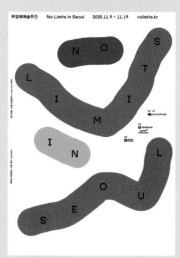

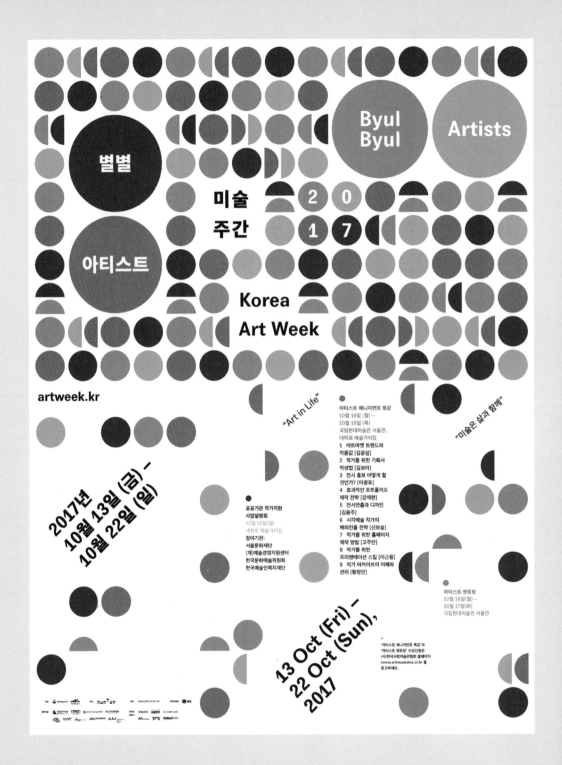

Korea Art Week 2017
___
Poster design for Korea Art Week
2017

Son Ayong

A Winter Watermelon. Poster design for the Jeonju International Film Festival. 2019.

**겨울의 수박 A WINTER WATERMELON
감독 DIRECTOR
황유정 HWANG YU-JUNG**

From South Korea

sonayong.com

Goods is Good

Poster design for an exhibition
2019

→
Goods is Good

Animated poster for an exhibition
2019

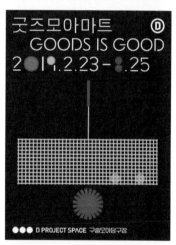

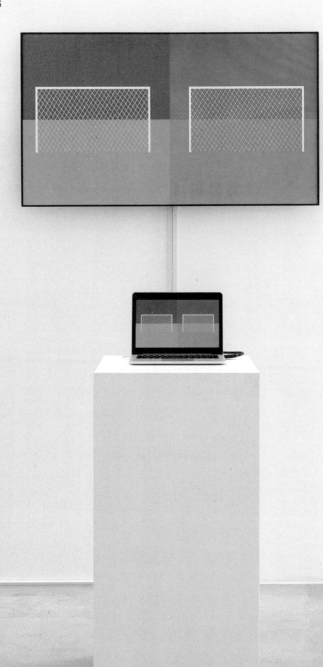

Background
—
Exhibition installation
2019

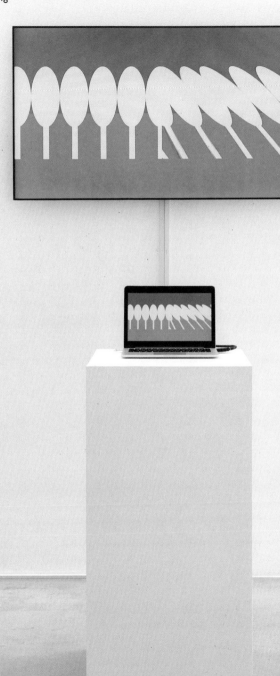

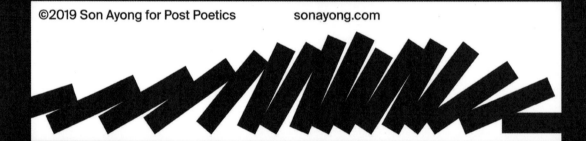

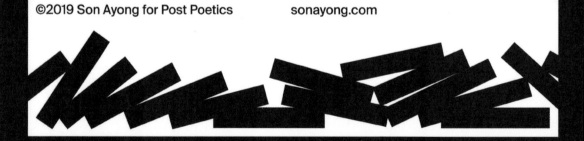

Post Poetics
___
Book mark designs for an art book distributor and bookstore
2019

Na Kim

SET v.9: patterns. Installation that forms part of an ongoing series titled SET, 2017.

From South Korea

ynkim.com

SET v.2: cover, pages
Installation that forms part of an ongoing series titled SET.
2016

SET
—
Various installations that form part of an ongoing series titled SET
2016–2019

Table A

Tables designed to correspond to
the different sizes of the 'A' series
of paper: A4, A3, A2, A1 and A0
2013

→
ÅLAND Brooklyn

Space design for a fashion store
2018

Na Kim

Bottomless Bag
Solo exhibition
2020

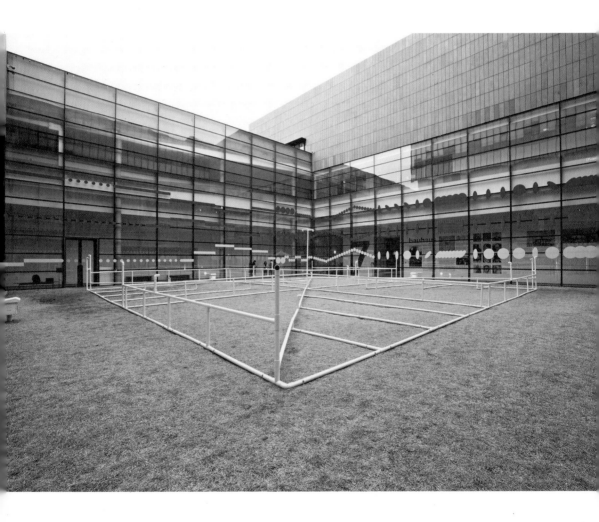

2'13", 36 Frames

Installation for the MMCA exhibition Human—Space—Machine. Stage Experiments at the Bauhaus.
2014

GRAPHIC

KIOSK
FORMS OF INQUIRY
KINROSS, MODERN TYPO-
GRAPHY (1992, 2004, 2009)
IN REAL LIFE
FROM MARS
PLACE IT
DESIGNING CRITICAL DESIGN
VISUAL POETRY KUMGANGSAN
ROMA PUBLICATIONS 1—90
EXTENDED CAPTION (DDDG)
GRAPHIC DESIGN
IN THE WHITE CUBE
ON PURPOSE

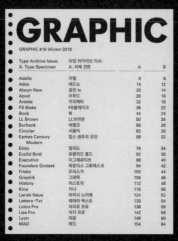

GRAPHIC
De Best
Verzorgde
Boeken
Les plus
beaux livres
français
Die schönsten
Schweizer
Bücher
Svensk
Bokkonst

GRAPHIC

Art direction for a magazine

Paika

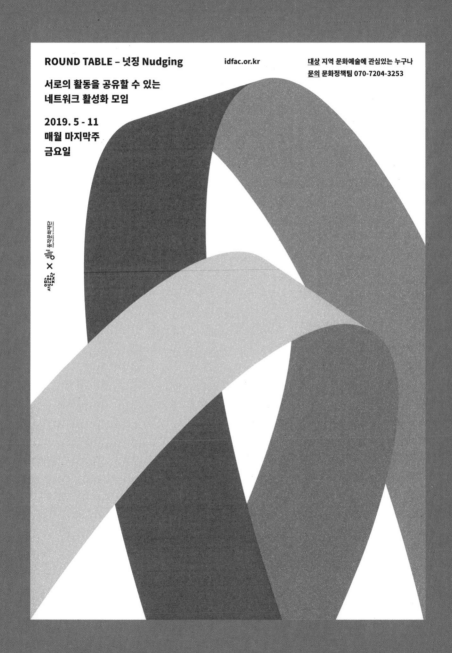

ROUND TABLE – 넛징 Nudging

서로의 활동을 공유할 수 있는
네트워크 활성화 모임

2019. 5 - 11
매월 마지막주
금요일

idfac.or.kr

대상 지역 문화예술에 관심있는 누구나
문의 문화정책팀 070-7204-3253

From South Korea

paika.org

주최
출판도시문화재단

후원 문화체육관광부
한국출판문화산업진흥원

2019 출판도시
인문학당

www.immunclub.org

inmunclub 2019

Poster design for cultural
foundation Paju Book City
2019

Paika

←

Yeongdeungpo Network Art Festival
Poster design for a festival
2020

A Story Haven't Heard or Seen
Poster design for Seoul Cultural
Foundation
2018

Open Warehouse
Poster design for Samil-ro
Changgo Theater
2019

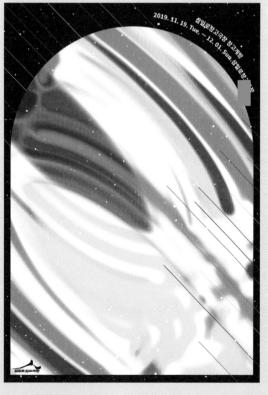

Against the Dragon Light
Logo design for a socially-engaged practice
2020

Corners Studio

Hansol Paper. Book design for a paper company. 2020.

From South Korea

corners.kr

Paper and Stencil Printing

Hansol Paper
Book design for a paper company
2020

가지   11

Somewhere Between Silkscreen and Offset Printing

P.9

‡ 실크 스크린 인쇄와 오프셋 인쇄 사이 어딘가에 ‡

조효준—코우너스

이고르

아루미 & 다니엘 비슈 (리소트립 프린트 숍, 리우데자네이루, 브라질) Igor Arume & Daniel Bicho (Risotrip Print Shop Co., Rio de Janeiro, Brazil) ¶ 우리는 대체로 브라질 제지사 수자누 파펠 이 셀룰로지가 제조한 플렝 볼드 90g을 사용한다. 부담 없는 가격과 부드러운 질감, 촉감, 흡수력을 고려했을 때 브라질에서 스텐실 인쇄용으로 쓰기에 더할 나위 없는 종이다. 트레이 위에 떨어져도 잉크가 번지지 않는다. FSC 인증을 받은 이 옅은 황백색 종이는 브라질 출판업계에서도 널리 쓰인다. 우리는 이 종이를 항상 구비해둔다. 이는 브라질 스텐실 인쇄 스튜디오에서 가장 사랑받는 종이이기도 하다. ¶ 이탈리아 제지사 페드리고니의 컬러 플러스도 사용한다. 페드리고니는 멋진 색지들을 보유하고 있는데, 이는 주로 책 커버나 엽서, 포스터에 쓰인다. 최근에는 프랑스 제지사

린지

버크 & 서배스천 버크 (리졸브, 펜실베이니아, 미국) Lyndsey Burke & Sebastian Burke (Risolve, Pennsylvania, United States) ¶ 우리는 손쉽게 사용할 수 있는 비코팅지를 주로 쓴다. 가장 선호하는 제지사는 모호크와 프렌치 페이퍼 컴퍼니다. 이 미국 제지사 두 곳은 모두 환경친화적인 제지법을 실천하기 때문에 마음에 든다. 스텐실 인쇄는 매우 환경친화적인 작업이며 우리는 가능한 한 환경에 적은 영향을 미치려고 노력하고 있다. ¶ 우리는 종이를 필요한 크기로

42

제니

기트먼 & 제스지트 길 (컬러 코드, 토론토, 캐나다) Jenny Gitman & Jesjit Gill (Colour Code, Toronto, Canada) ¶ 우리는 돔타르, 모호크, 프렌치 페이퍼 컴퍼니의 종이를 주로 쓴다. 이 세 군데 제지사에서 생산하는 종이는 코팅되지 않았고 피지 느낌이 나며 거칠고 투박해 스텐실 인쇄에 적합하다. 지역 거래처를 통해, 또는 제지사에 직접 주문해 다양한 크기와 색상으로 구입할 수 있다. 시행착오를 거쳐 우리는 스텐실 잉크에 가장 알맞은 종이를 찾을 수 있었다. 스텐실 잉크는 종이에 흡수되면서 마르는데, 지난 6년간의 경험에 따르면 앞서 언급한 종이들이야말로 가장 믿을 만하고 만족스러운 결과물을 제공한다. 종이는 주문 후 익일 또는 업무일 기준

얀

디르크 더 빌더 & 조이스 휠레이 (크누스트, 나이메겐, 네덜란드) Jan Dirk de Wilde & Joyce Guley (Knust, Nijmegen, Netherlands) ¶ 우리는 대개 두께 1.5에서 2.0 사이, 80g에서 120g짜리 서적 용지인 매트한 종이를 사용한다. 거친 텍스트 용지, 커버 용지, 재생지를 좋아하고, 보통 120g에서 300g 사이, 또는 350g이나 400g을 사용한다. 판지나 신문 인쇄 용지, 크라프트지, 포장지로 쓰이는 종이를 사용하기도 한다. ¶ 종이가 두꺼울수록 불건성 스텐실 잉크를 잘 흡수하기 때문에 얇고 매끈한 종이에 비해 잉크가 덜 번지고 스텐실 인쇄기에 잘맞는다. 우리는 천이나 섬유

ii。 50g/m² 이하의 종이는 종이가 드럼 스텐실에 붙어 인쇄기 밖으로 나오지 않는 현상이 발생했다.

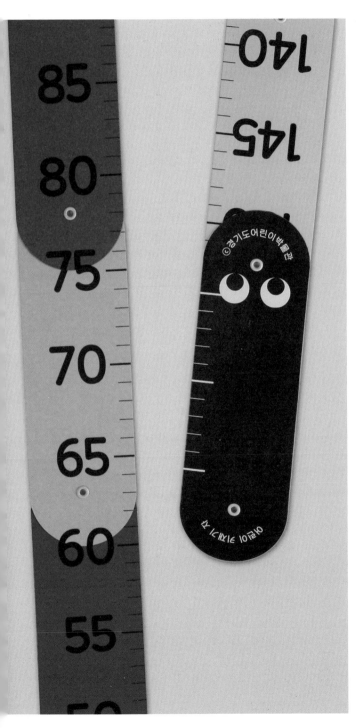

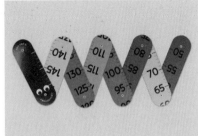

Gyeonggi Children's Museum

Merchandise for a children's museum
2018

헤겔의 변증법

스탠퍼드 철학백과의 항목들 7

전기가오리

9,900원
979-11-88319-03-9
979-11-958729-1-6 (세트)

Arko Art Center
Leaflet design for an art center
2018

Ordinary People

From South Korea

ordinarypeople.kr

Gamecon

Event identity for entertainment
and mass media company CJ ENM
2019

Uncommon Eyewear

Branding for a retailer of
prescription glasses and sunglasses
2019

→
Korean Gardens

Exhibition identity
2019

Korean Gardens
Exhibition identity
2019

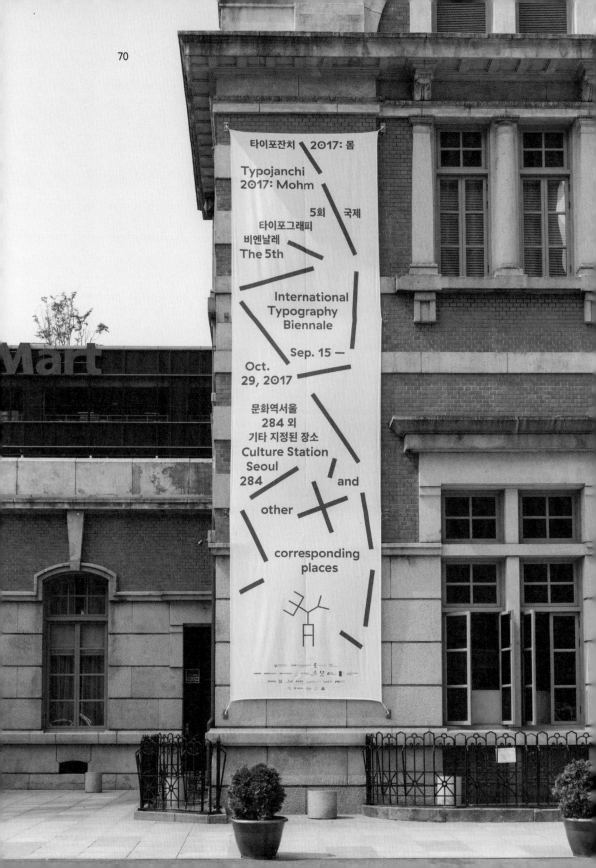

Ordinary People

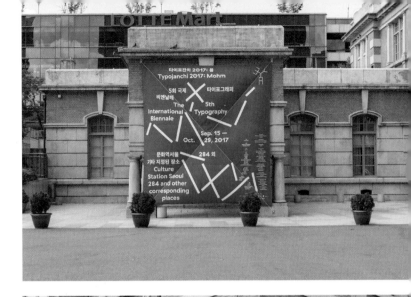

Typojanchi 2017 Mohm
Identity for an international
typography biennale
2017

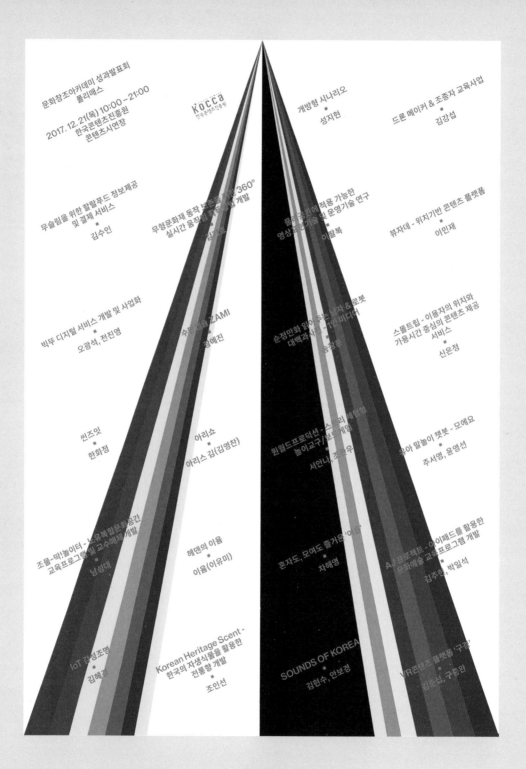

Polymath

Poster design for Korea Creative Content Agency
2019

Shin Dokho

Sunset Rollercoaster Live in Korea. Poster design in collaboration with Kyungho Ryu for Helicopter Records. 2018.

From South Korea

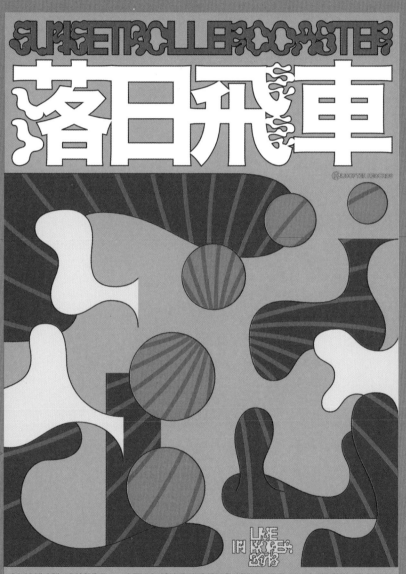

shindokho.kr

In Memory of Shin-Haechul

Book design for publishers
Dolbegae
2018

→
AAMP
Poster design for an artist collective
2019

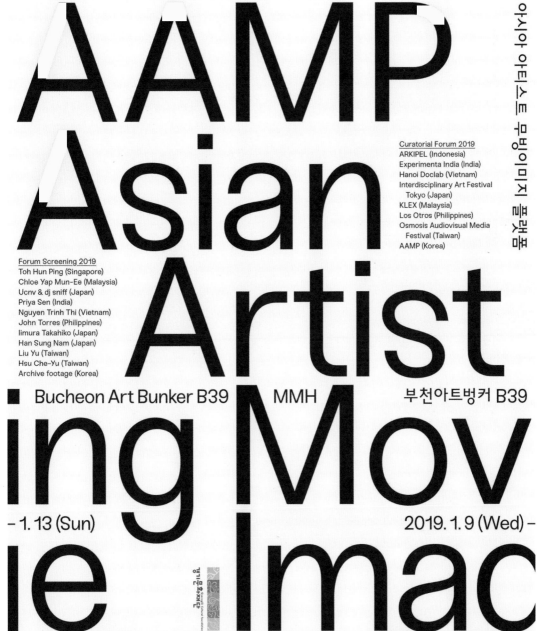

AAMP
Asian
Artist
ing Mov
je Imac
tform Pla

아시아 아티스트 무빙이미지 플랫폼

Curatorial Forum 2019
ARKIPEL (Indonesia)
Experimenta India (India)
Hanoi Doclab (Vietnam)
Interdisciplinary Art Festival
   Tokyo (Japan)
KLEX (Malaysia)
Los Otros (Philippines)
Osmosis Audiovisual Media
   Festival (Taiwan)
AAMP (Korea)

Forum Screening 2019
Toh Hun Ping (Singapore)
Chloe Yap Mun-Ee (Malaysia)
Ucnv & dj sniff (Japan)
Priya Sen (India)
Nguyen Trinh Thi (Vietnam)
John Torres (Philippines)
Iimura Takahiko (Japan)
Han Sung Nam (Japan)
Liu Yu (Taiwan)
Hsu Che-Yu (Taiwan)
Archive footage (Korea)

Bucheon Art Bunker B39   MMH   부천아트벙커 B39

– 1. 13 (Sun)   2019. 1. 9 (Wed) –

DIE GEDANKEN SIND FREI

LIEDBASEL
23. Mai – 26. Mai 2019
Ackermannshof

LIEDBasel entstand aus Liederabenden in Basler Wohnzimmern. Bei Wein und Gesang wuchs die Idee, die einzelnen Gastgeber und Liedbegeisterten zusammenzubringen und einen Austausch zu fördern. Das Kunstlied und das Format Liederabend sollen wieder feste Grösse in der Basler Hausmusik werden. Gleichzeitig bilden die FREUNDE ein musikalisches und finanzielles Netz und sind damit die wichtigste Säule im Festival LIEDBasel. Der Enthusiasmus der FREUNDE ist für die Grundstimmung des Festivals entscheidend.

LIEDBasel
———
Poster design for an international
music festival
2019

→
Siwon Kim
———
Poster design for an artist
2020

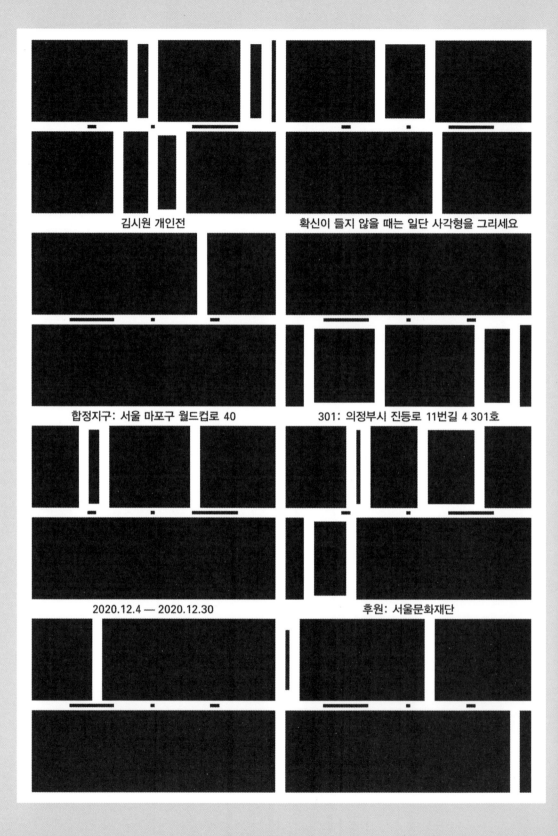

김시원 개인전

확신이 들지 않을 때는 일단 사각형을 그리세요

합정지구: 서울 마포구 월드컵로 40

301: 의정부시 진등로 11번길 4 301호

2020.12.4 — 2020.12.30

후원: 서울문화재단

Sulki and Min

Graphic West 7: Yellow Pages. Poster design for DNP Foundation for Cultural Promotion and DDD Gallery. 2018.

From South Korea

sulki-min.com

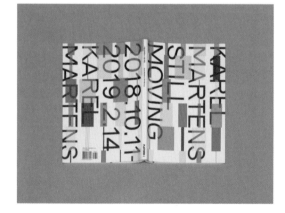

Karel Martens: Still Moving

Catalogue design for Platform-L Contemporary
Art Center
2018

Photography by Kim Kyoungtae

KAREL
MARTENS
STILL
MOVING

카렐 마르턴스: 스틸 무빙

Karel Martens: Still Moving

2018.10.11–
2018.12.11

PLATFORM-L

MMCA Performing Arts
Poster designs for the National
Museum of Modern and
Contemporary Art
2017–2018

→
Publishing as Method
Poster design for The Book Society
and Art Sonje Center
2020

Kedai-Kedai Merdeka typeface
designed by Huruf, Kuala Lumpur

PUBLISHING

아트선재센터
2020년 10월 30일~12월 20일

라이팅 밴드
류한길
민구홍 매뉴팩처링
슬기와 민
윤지원
진 쿱
카이파 타
후팡

기획
임경용

공동 연구
현시원

방법으로서의 출판

ART SONJE CENTER
OCT. 30–DEC. 20, 2020

HU FANG
KAYFA TA
MINGUHONG MANUFACTURING
RYU HANKIL
SULKI & MIN
WRITING BAND
YOON JEEWON
ZINE COOP

CURATED BY
LIM KYUNG YONG

RESEARCH COLLABORATION
HYUN SEEWON

AS
METHOD

주최
아트선재센터
더 북 소사이어티

후원
한국문화예술위원회
예술경영지원센터

CO-HOSTED BY
ART SONJE CENTER
THE BOOK SOCIETY

SUPPORTED BY
ARTS COUNCIL KOREA
KOREA ARTS MANAGEMENT SERVICE

A   SJ   C

Ungmang

Banner design for Ilmin Museum of Art

2018

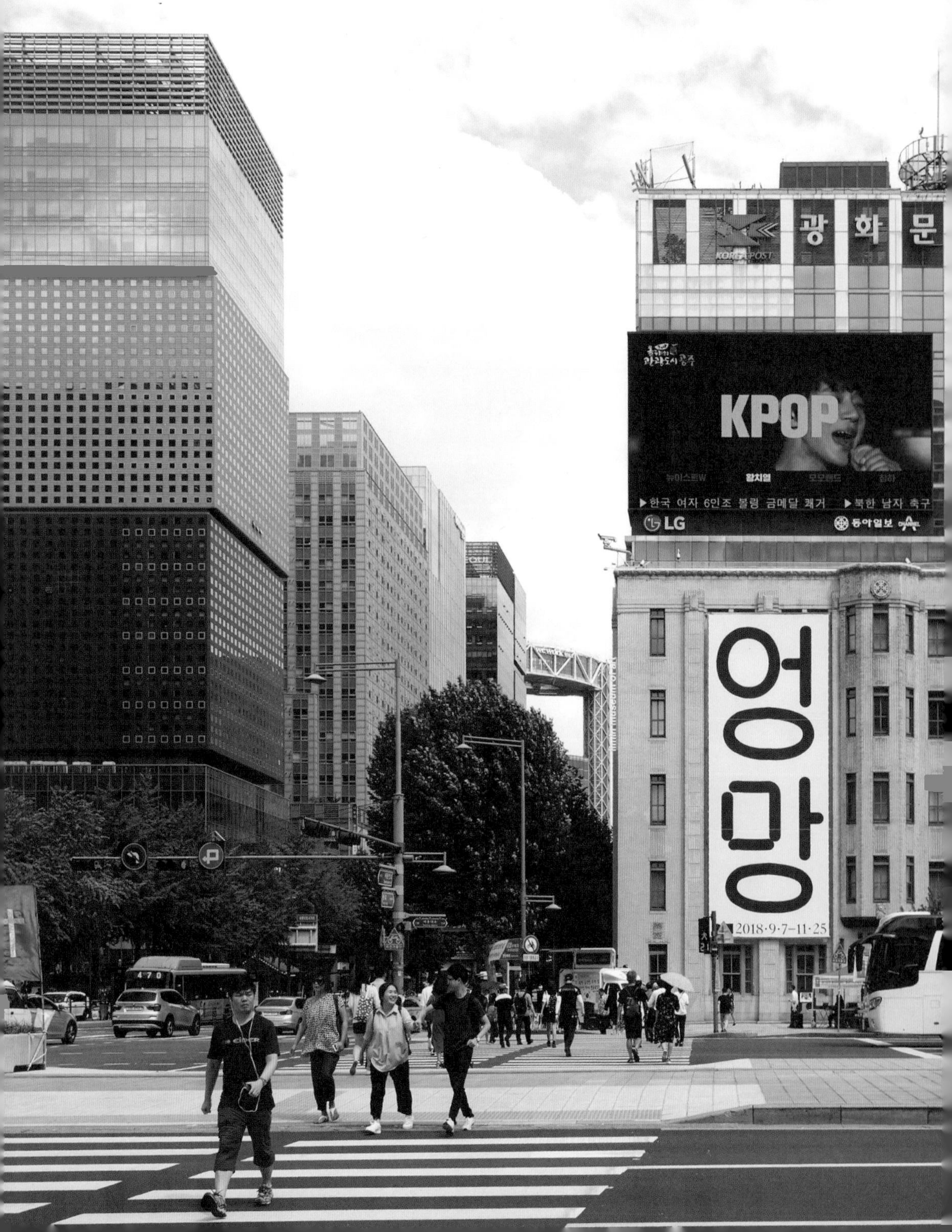

Graphic West 9: Sulki & Min

京都dddギャラリー第227回企画展　2021年1月16日（土）－3月19日（金）
kyoto ddd gallery The 227th Exhibition　16 January–19 March 2021

主催：公益財団法人 DNP文化振興財団　キュレーター：後藤哲也
Organized by DNP Foundation for Cultural Promotion　Curated by Tetsuya Goto

---

Graphic West 9: Sulki & Min

Poster design for DNP Foundation for Cultural Promotion and DDD Gallery

2021

BOWYER

From South Korea

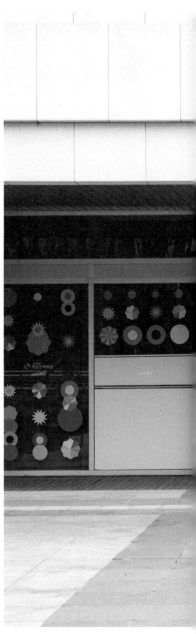

Sejong Center, New Year Graphic

Installation design for an art center

2015

서울마블러스평양
평양판타스틱서울
서브릴리언톄양
서울 오섬 평양
일럼스트리어숀
평양스페셜서울
평매그니피센트울

서울♥내일만나요♥평양
Seoul♥SeeYouTomorrow♥Pyeongyang
9.17 – 9.26, 2018
DDP 둘레길

주최 서울특별시
주관 서울디자인재단

Seoul ♥ SeeYouTomorrow ♥ Pyeongyang
Exhibition identity design for Seoul City, Seoul Design Foundation
2018

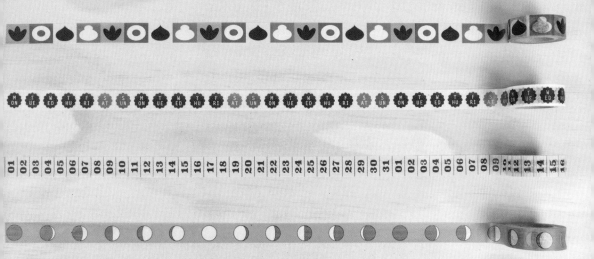

Time to Tape

Tape design for the 2017
Gwangju Design Biennale –
Gardener's Market
2017

Welcome! You Are Connected

Exhibition identity and catalogue design
for Suwon Museum of Art
2019

Cup of Coffee
Catalogue cover design for the exhibition 'Cup of Coffee' at 63art
2018

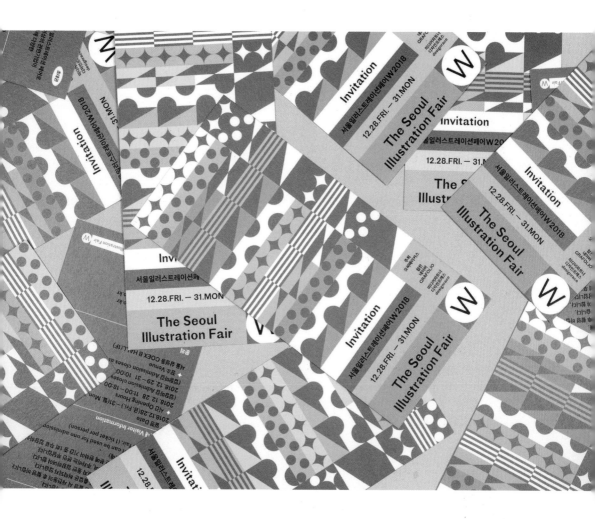

The Seoul Illustration Fair 2018

Exhibition identity for an illustration fair
2018

Ghidam
Visual identity for public art project Ghidam
2020

Jin & Park

A Dwarf Launches a Little Ball. Poster design for Gallery Woomul. 2017

From South Korea

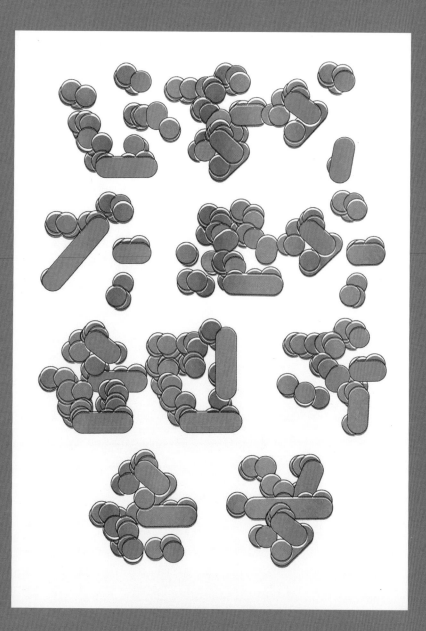

jinandpark.com

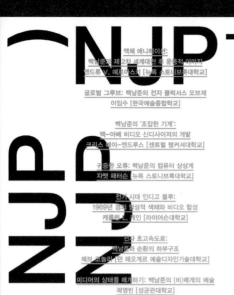

경기도박물관 대강당
2016.9.9 금
11:00–18:00

국제학술심포지엄
백남준의 선물
⑧
NJP를
다시 움직이기:
백남준의
인터페이스들

액체 애니메이션:
백남준과 제 2차 세계대전 후 운동적 이미지
앤드류 V. 예로슈키 [뉴욕 스토니브룩대학교]

글로벌 그루브: 백남준의 전자 콜렉서스 오브제
이일수 [한국예술종합학교]

백남준의 '조잡한 기계':
백-아베 비디오 신디사이저의 개발
크리스 메이-앤드루스 [센트럴 랭커셔대학교]

귀중한 오류: 백남준의 컴퓨터 상상계
자넷 패터슨 [뉴욕 스토니브룩대학교]

전기 시대 인디고 블루:
1969년 경의 합성적 색채와 비디오 합성
캐롤린 케인 [라이어슨대학교]

전자 초고속도로:
백남준와 순환의 하부구조
매브 코놀리 [던 래오게르 예술디자인기술대학교]

미디어의 상태를 매개하기: 백남준의 (비)매개의 예술
곽영빈 [성균관대학교]

사회 및 종합토론:
김지훈 [중앙대학교], 김희영 [국민대학교],
안경화 [백남준아트센터], 오경은 [이화여자대학교],
정영실 [홍익대학교], 발표자들

주최 및 주관: 백남준아트센터, 경기문화재단
기획: 김지훈
상세 내용 www.njpartcenter.kr 문의 031 201 8551

Reanimating NJP:
Nam June Paik's Interfaces
Exhibition identity for the Nam June
Paik Art Center
2016

101

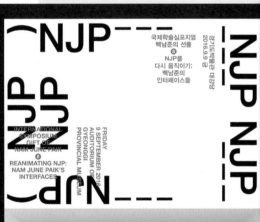

color study 2015.7.29—10.23 savina museum

savina museum of
contemporary art
www.savinamuseum.com

Bernard Faucon
HYBE
Hyungmin Moon
Jin Dallae & Park Woohyuk
Juhae Yong
MeeNa Park
Neil Harbisson
Sandy Skoglund
Seung Jung
Sohee Cho

Collaborated with
Play Makers Lab,
Graduate School of
Communication & Arts,
Yonsei University/
Color Lab,
Department of
Industrial Design,
KAIST

Supported by Arts Council Korea
Sponsored by Renova, Doosung Paper

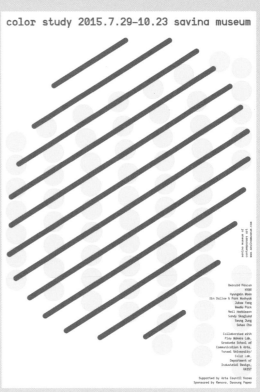

Color Study
Poster designs for Savina Museum
2015

→
Gwangju Media Art Festival
Poster design for Gwangju Media
Art Festival
2018

G — MAF 2018
G — MAF 2018
G — MAF 2018
G — MAF 2018
G — MAF 2018
G — MAF 2018
G — MAF 2018

GWANGJU MEDIA ART FESTIVAL
GWANGJU MEDIA ART FESTIVAL
GWANGJU MEDIA ART FESTIVAL
GWANGJU MEDIA ART FEST
GWANGJU MEDIA

2018.11.28. - 12.07.
2018.11.28. - 12.07.
2018.11.28. - 12.07.

THE BIRTH OF MACHINE-GOD
ALGORITHMIC SOCIETY : THE BIRTH OF MACHINE-GOD
ALGORITHMIC SOCIETY : THE BIRTH OF
ALGORITHMIC SOCIETY :
ALGORITHMIC

2018 광주
미디어아트페스티벌

알고리즘 소사이어티 :
기계—신의 탄생

국립아시아문화전당
복합2관+미디어월

주최
광주광역시
국립아시아문화전당

주관
광주문화재단
아시아문화원

ASIA CULTURE CENTER (ACC)
SPACE 2 & MEDIA WALL

HOST
GWANGJU METROPOLITAN CITY
ASIA CULTURE CENTER

ORGANIZER
GWANGJU CULTURAL FOUNDATION
ASIA CULTURE INSTITUTE

G — MAF 2018
G — MAF 2018
G — MAF 2018
G — MAF 2018
G — MAF 2018
G — MAF 2018
G — MAF 2018

MEDIA ART FESTIVAL
GWANGJU MEDIA ART FESTIVAL
GWANGJU MEDIA ART FEST
GWANGJU MEDIA

THE BIRTH OF MACHINE-GOD : ALGORITHMIC SOCIETY
ALGORITHMIC SOCIETY : THE BIRTH
ALGORITHMIC

2018. 11. 28. – 2018. 12. 07.

2018 광주
미디어아트페스티벌

알고리즘 소사이어티 :
기계–신의 탄생

국립아시아문화전당
복합2관+미디어월

주최
광주광역시
국립아시아문화전당

주관
광주문화재단
아시아문화원

ASIA CULTURE CENTER (ACC)
SPACE 2 & MEDIA WALL

HOST
GWANGJU METROPOLITAN CITY
ASIA CULTURE CENTER

ORGANIZER
GWANGJU CULTURAL FOUNDATION
ASIA CULTURE INSTITUTE

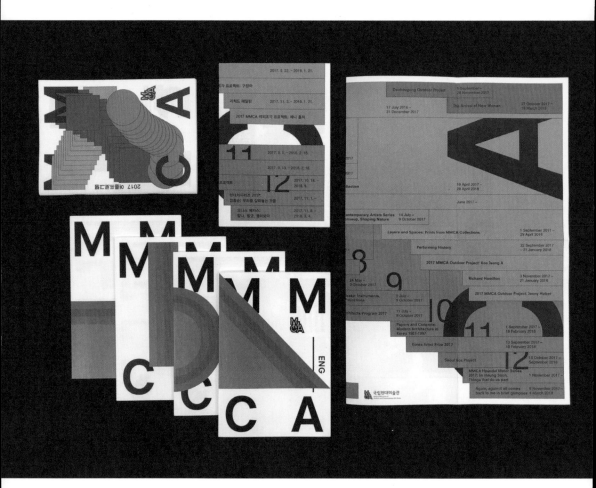

MMCA

Program booklet for the National
Museum of Modern and
Contemporary Art
2017

Triangle

From South Korea

triangle-studio.co.kr

Triangle

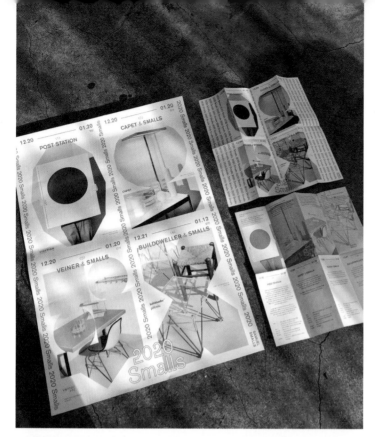

2020 Smalls
—
Identity for an achive exhibition
2020

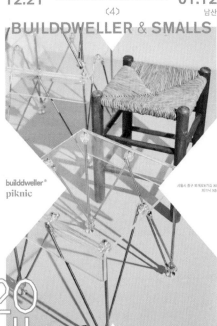

12.20 ———————— **01.20**
〈1〉 청담
POST STATION

STAYTION
CHEONGDAM 점

지하철 7호선 청담역 4번 3층
STAYTION 청담

12.20 ———————— **01.20**
〈2〉 망원
CAPET & SMALLS

CAPET

서울시 마포구 동교로 9길 72
1층 카펫 망원

12.20 ———————— **01.20**
〈3〉 신사
VEINER & SMALLS

veiner
:snc

서울시 강남구 강남대로156길
2층 베이너

12.21 ———————— **01.12**
〈4〉 남산
BUILDDWELLER & SMALLS

builddweller ®
piknic

서울시 중구 퇴계로6가길 30
피크닉 3층

SAMUEL
SMALLS

2020
Smalls

DMZ Peace Train Music Festival

Identity for a music festival

2019

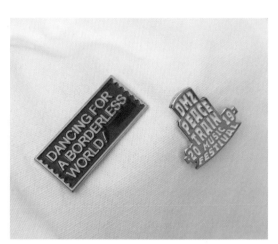

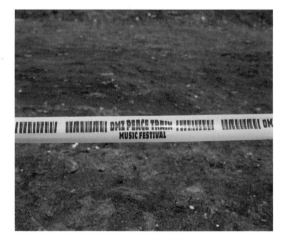

Bupyeong Cultural Foundation
2017 Season Package
Catalogue design for a cultural foundation
2017

Oh! CREATOR X SWNA
Art book design
2018

CFC

A Twosome Place. Branding for a coffee franchise. 2020.

From South Korea

contentformcontext.com

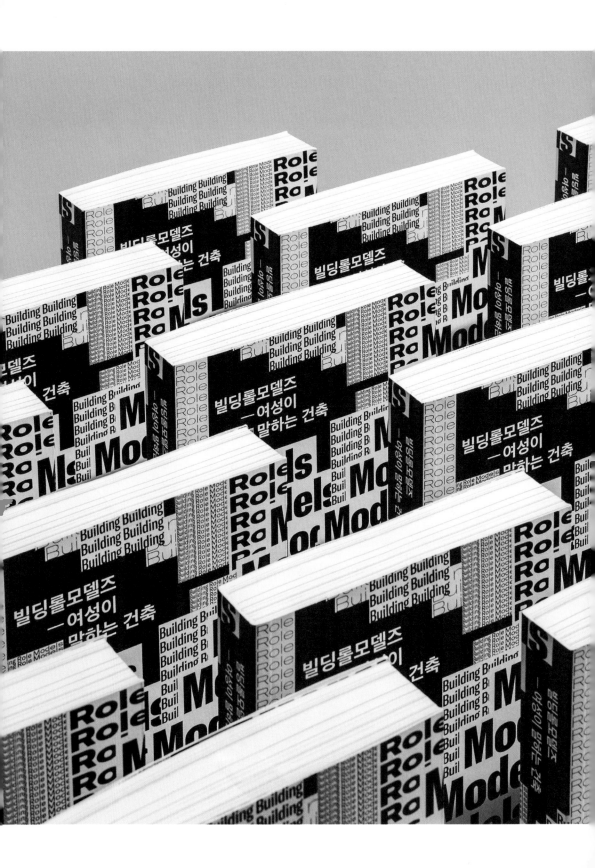

←
Building Role Models
___

Seminar identity and book design
2019

Beauty Point Week
___

Identity design for a beauty event
2018

→
Apartmentary
___

Branding for an apartment
remodeling service platform
2020

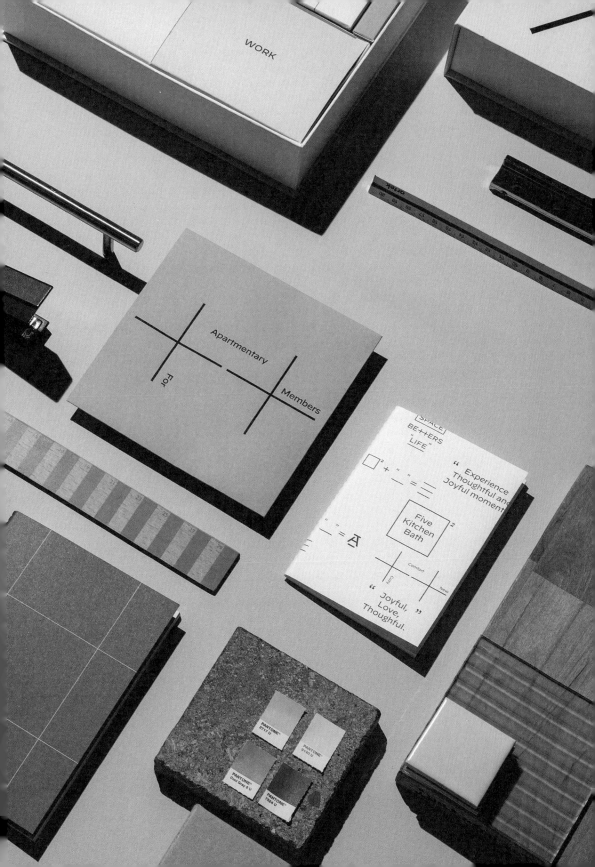

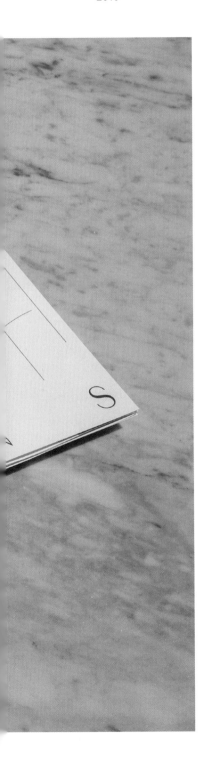

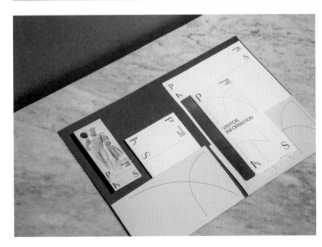

Love the Earth
Campaign identity for Primera
2019

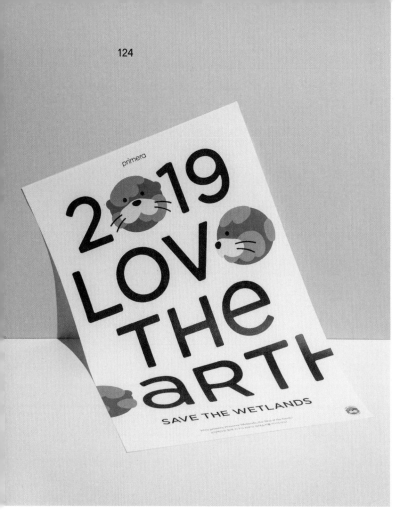

Everyday Practice

ACC
5th Anniversary

2020
ACC_R
Residency
Exhibition

국립아시아문화전당
개관 5주년 기념

2020
ACC_R
레지던시
결과 전시

BIO
PHILIA
바이오필리아

A
HANDFUL OF
EARTH

흙
한줌의
우주

Asia
Culture
Center
ACC Creation
Space 1

국립아시아
문화전당
문화창조원
복합1관

2020.11.24–
2021.03.01

Organized by
Asia Culture Center

Produced by
Asia Culture Institute

Asia Culture Center
38 Munhwajeondang-ro,
Dong-gu, Gwangju 61485,
Republic of Korea

T. 1899-5666
www.acc.go.kr

주최 국립아시아문화전당

주관 아시아문화원

국립아시아문화전당 동구 문화전당로 38

T. 1899-5666
www.acc.go.kr

From South Korea

everyday-practice.com

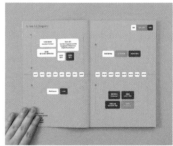

C-lab4.0 UN+CONTACT

Catalogue design for
an art museum
2020

The Arium
Catalogue design for the Seoul
Women's Craft Center
2020

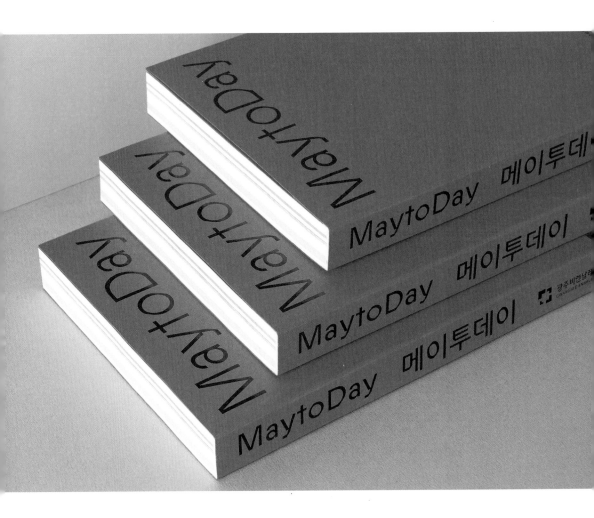

MaytoDay
Catalogue design for the Gwangju Biennale
2020

Here, Here is People
Book design for the publisher Humannitas
2020

The Institutional Theory: A Protean Creature
Book design for the publisher Philoelectroray
2020

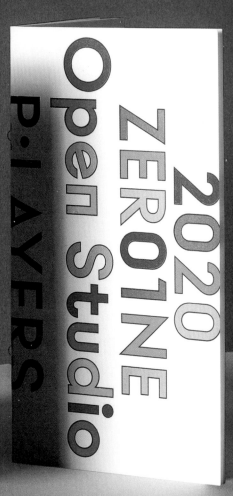

ZER01NE Open Studio

Leaflet design for an art residence

2020

→

Time Lost, Time Registered

Identity design for an exhibition

2020

경기관광공사
Gyeonggi Tourism Organization

TIME LOST | TIME REGAINED

www.dmzcamp131.or.kr

두 개의   TIME LOST,   경기도 파주시 군내면 백연리 357-1
시간   TIME REGAINED   캠프그리브스 '갤러리 그리브스'

Hezin O

From South Korea

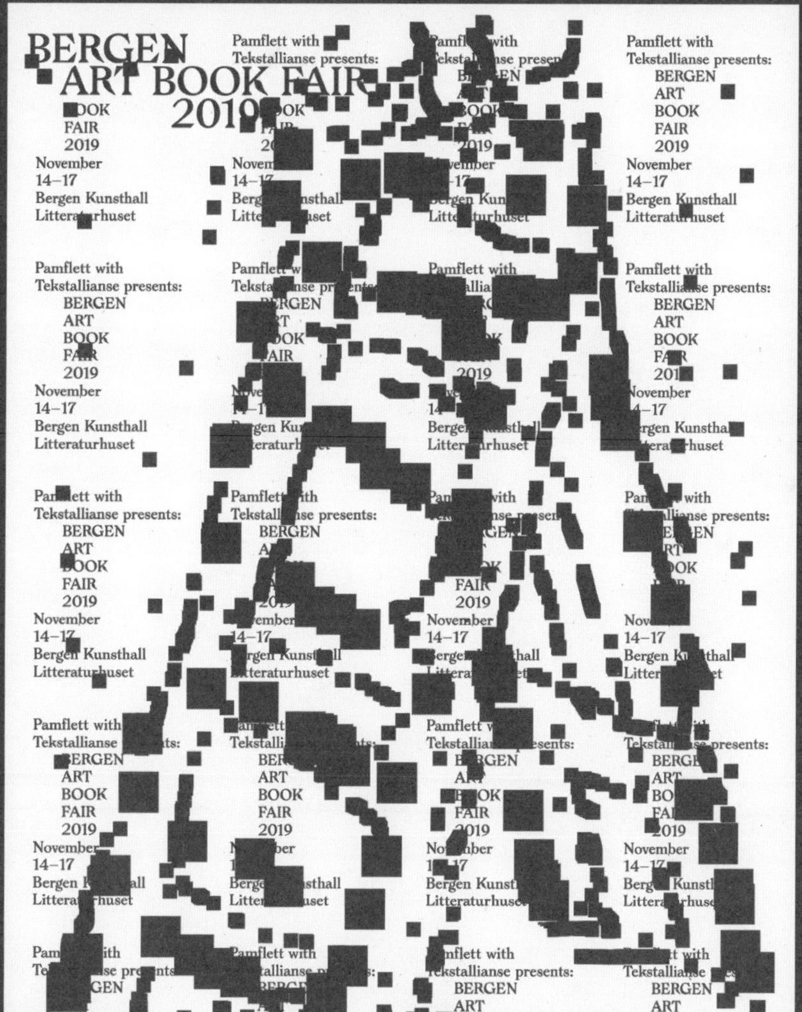

BERGEN ART BOOK FAIR 2019

Pamflett with Tekstallianse presents: BERGEN ART BOOK FAIR 2019
November 14–17
Bergen Kunsthall
Litteraturhuset

Pamflett with Tekstallianse presents: BERGEN ART BOOK FAIR 2019
November 14–17
Bergen Kunsthall
Litteraturhuset

Pamflett with Tekstallianse presents: BERGEN ART BOOK FAIR 2019
November 14–17
Bergen Kunsthall
Litteraturhuset

Pamflett with Tekstallianse presents: BERGEN ART BOOK FAIR 2019
November 14–17
Bergen Kunsthall
Litteraturhuset

NOVEMBER 14–17
BERGEN KUNSTHALL
LITTERATURHUSET

BERGEN ART BOOK FAIR 2019

BOOK FAIR 2019
November 14–17
Bergen Kunsthall
Litteraturhuset

Pamflett with Tekstallianse presents:
BERGEN ART BOOK FAIR 2019
November 14–17
Bergen Kunsthall
Litteraturhuset

Pamflett with Tekstallianse presents:
BERGEN ART BOOK FAIR 2019
November 14–17
Bergen Kunsthall
Litteraturhuset

Pamflett with Tekstallianse presents:
BERGEN ART BOOK FAIR 2019
November 14–17
Bergen Kunsthall
Litteraturhuset

Pamflett with Tekstallianse presents:
BERGEN ART BOOK FAIR 2019
November 14–17
Bergen Kunsthall
Litteraturhuset

Pamflett with Tekstallianse presents:
BERGEN ART BOOK FAIR 2019
November 14–17
Bergen Kunsthall
Litteraturhuset

Pamflett with Tekstallianse presents:
BERGEN ART BOOK FAIR 2019
November 14–17
Bergen Kunsthall
Litteraturhuset

Pamflett with Tekstallianse presents:
BERGEN ART BOOK FAIR 2019
November 14–17
Bergen Kunsthall
Litteraturhuset

Pamflett with Tekstallianse presents:
BERGEN ART BOOK FAIR 2019
November 14–17
Bergen Kunsthall
Litteraturhuset

Pamflett with Tekstallianse presents:
BERGEN ART BOOK FAIR 2019
November 14–17
Bergen Kunsthall
Litteraturhuset

Pamflett with Tekstallianse presents:
BERGEN ART BOOK FAIR 2019
November 14–17
Bergen Kunsthall
Litteraturhuset

Pamflett with Tekstallianse presents:
BERGEN ART BOOK FAIR 2019
November 14–17
Bergen Kunsthall
Litteraturhuset

Pamflett with Tekstallianse presents:
BERGEN ART BOOK FAIR 2019
November 14–17
Bergen Kunsthall
Litteraturhuset

Pamflett with Tekstallianse presents:
BERGEN ART BOOK FAIR 2019
November 14–17
Bergen Kunsthall
Litteraturhuset

Pamflett with Tekstallianse presents:
BERGEN ART BOOK FAIR 2019
November 14–17
Bergen Kunsthall
Litteraturhuset

Pamflett with Tekstallianse presents:
BERGEN ART BOOK FAIR 2019
November 14–17
Bergen Kunsthall
Litteraturhuset

NOVEMBER 14–17
BERGEN KUNSTHALL
LITTERATURHUSET

The House H
———
Branding for a department store
2020

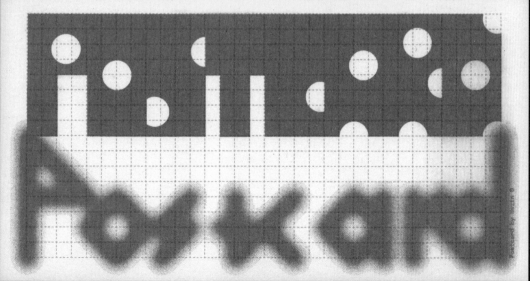

Born, A Woman
Editorial design for Suwon Museum of Art
2020

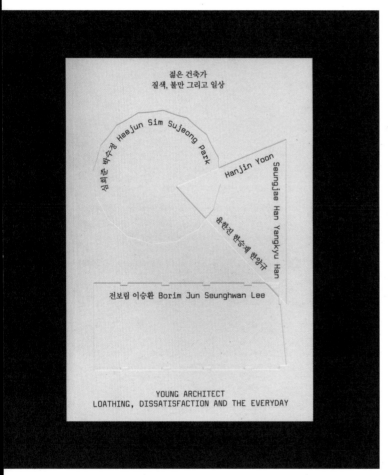

Young Architect: Loathing, Dissatisfaction and the Everyday

Book design for the Korea Architect Institute

2019

DDBBMM

Rest Forest. Identity design for a cultural institution. 2019.

From South Korea

ddbbmm.kr

Midnight in Seoul
Brochure design for a city observatory
2016

→
Drawing Busan: Haeundae

Poster for Busan Art Book Fair
2019

→
Tone Studio Live 3

Poster design for a concert hall
2018

DADA Factory
Poster design for Seongbuk
Children's Museum
2019

Peppertones Club Tour
Poster design for a music company
2019

→
ACC Academy
Poster design for the Asia
Culture Center
2017

기간: 2017. 3-6.
장소: 국립아시아문화전당 문화정보원
개강: 2017. 3. 28 (화)
신청: 2017. 3. 2 (목)부터 홈페이지 접수

수강신청: www.acc.go.kr
문의: 1899-5566
주최: 국립아시아문화전당
주관: 아시아문화원

2017 상반기
국립아시아문화전당
ACC 아카데미

문화적 상상력의 뿌리를 찾아서
06 / 01 아카데미실 B

고전읽기: 혼돈의 시대에 장자를 읽다
07

일러스트레이션

라이브클래식 III
03 / 28
20 / 극장 3

음악순례 III: 애니메이션에서 현대음악까지
06 / 12
14 / 아카데미실 B

현대적 고전을 찾아서 III 사랑과 문학

시네마 천국 III: 사랑에 대한

음악순례 III: 메이션에서 음악까지

고전읽기: 혼돈의 시대에 자를 읽다
미실 C

아시아 철학

스튜디오

그림책 스튜디오
05 / 18 아카데미실 A

예술夜: 인문(人文)적 인간을 위한 문학
04 / 05
26 / 아카데미실 B

예술夜, 그 곳의 음악
04 / 25 아카데미실 B

예술夜: 미술을 는가

2017 상반기 국립아시아문화전당 ACC 아카데미

미술관에 가고 싶어지는 미술사 이야기
04 / 06
12 / 07 아카데미실

일상의 예술, 디자인과 공예 이야기
13

라이브클래식 III
03 / 28
20 / 극장 3

예술夜: 영화는 미술을 어떻게 이용하는가
04 / 22 아카데미실 A

예술夜: 아시아, 그 곳의 음악
05 / 05
25 / 아카데미실 B

고전읽기: 혼돈의 시대에 장자를 읽

미술관에 가고 싶어지는 미술사 이야기
04 / 06
12 / 07 아카데미실 A

시네마 천국 III: 사랑에 대한 모든 것
03 / 28

그림책 스튜디오
미실 A

예술夜: 아시아, 그 곳의 음악
05 / 05
04 / 25 아카데미실

라이브클래식 III
03 / 06
20 / 극장 3

Noryang Battle
Poster design for GRAPHIC Magazine
2019

Jaehoon Choi

From South Korea

PARANOID PARK

Fig.01

Fig.02

YOUNG ARTIST OPEN CALL 2019
FEBRUARY.20.TO.FEBRUARY.24.
COEX C HALL

Fig.03

Fig.04

Fig.05

KIM DANIEL · KIM MINHEE · ROH YOUNGMEE
PARK SOHYUN · PARK JUNGHAE · PARK JIAE
WOO JEONGSU · LEE KANGHYUK · LEE MIJUNG
LEE JIYEON · CHEON · HAM SUNGJU

Fig.06

Fig.07

Fig.08

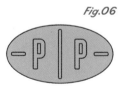

CURATED BY YOO JINSANG & YOON JULI
ORGANIZED & MANAGED BY
GALLERIES ASSOCIATION OF KOREA

werkgraphic.com

1924-76

The material for "Casserole and Ciesed Mussels, Mussel shells", 1964.

DESCRIPTION
OVER THE COURSE OF 12 EXTRAORDINARY YEARS, MARCEL BROODTHAERS DEVELOPED A DISTINCTIVE BODY OF WORK. ONE THAT ANTICIPATED MANY OF THE CONCERNS OF CONCEPTUAL ART. BORN IN BRUSSELS, BROODTHAERS WORKED PRIMARILY AS A POET UNTIL THE AGE OF 40. IN 1964, HE ANNOUNCED AN ENTRY INTO THE VISUAL ARTS BY TRANSFORMING THE UNSOLD COPIES OF HIS LAST POETRY BOOK INTO A SCULPTURE. THE IDEA BEHIND THIS GESTURE, NAMELY THE CONNECTION BETWEEN OBJECTS THAT HE HAD FIRST USED IN POETIC VERSE, HIS EARLY ARTWORKS DID NOT REPRESENT HIS TURN AWAY FROM POETRY BUT RATHER HIS EFFORT TO GIVE IT MATERIAL FORM.

M.B.

EXTENSION		ORIGIN / NATION	
Conceptual Arts		Belgian	
NAME		PERIOD	
Marcel Broodthaers		20th century	

NOTABLE WORKS
TAPIS DE SABLE (1974)
FÉMUR D HOMME BELGE & FÉMUR DE LA FEMME FRANCAISE (1965)
CASSEROLE AND CLOSED MUSSELS, MUSSEL SHELLS (1964)

M   MM>DD>YYYY
    01>28>1924
    Ulan>500004693

NOUS N'IRONS PLUS AU BOIS LES LAURIERS SONT NE SONT PAS COUPES

a̸ ✂ a̸ ✂ a̸

FÉMUR D'HOMME BELGE & FÉMUR DE LA FEMME FRANCAISE

a̸ ✂ a̸ ✂ a̸

CASSEROLE AND CLOSED MUSSELS, MUSSEL SHELLS

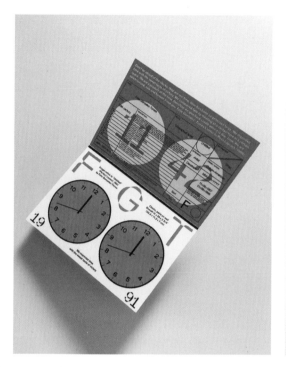

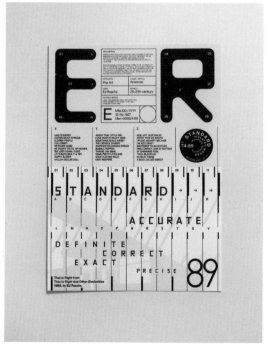

Double
Self-initiated project
2020

Studio Simdo
Identity for a photography studio
2020

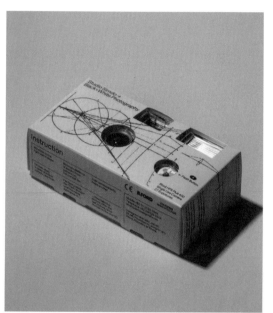

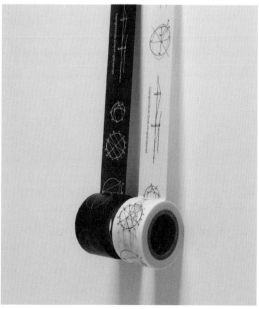

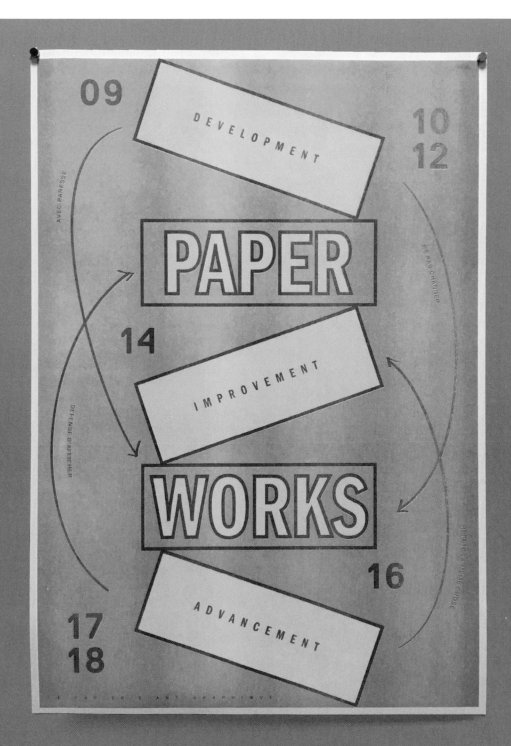

6699press

POPOCOMI. Book cover design. 2020.

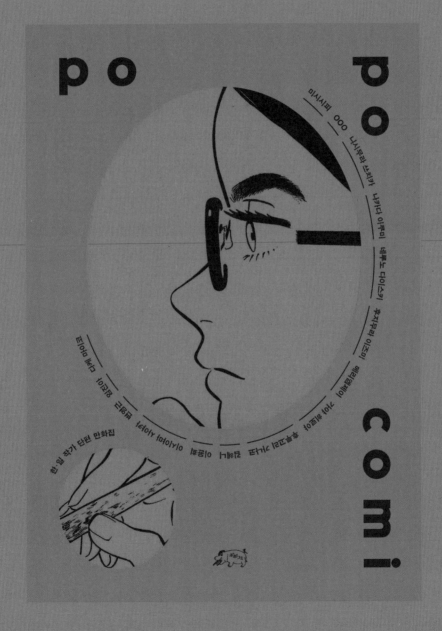

From South Korea

Diaspora Film Festival
———
Identity for a film festival
2016

Illustration by Jeewook Choi

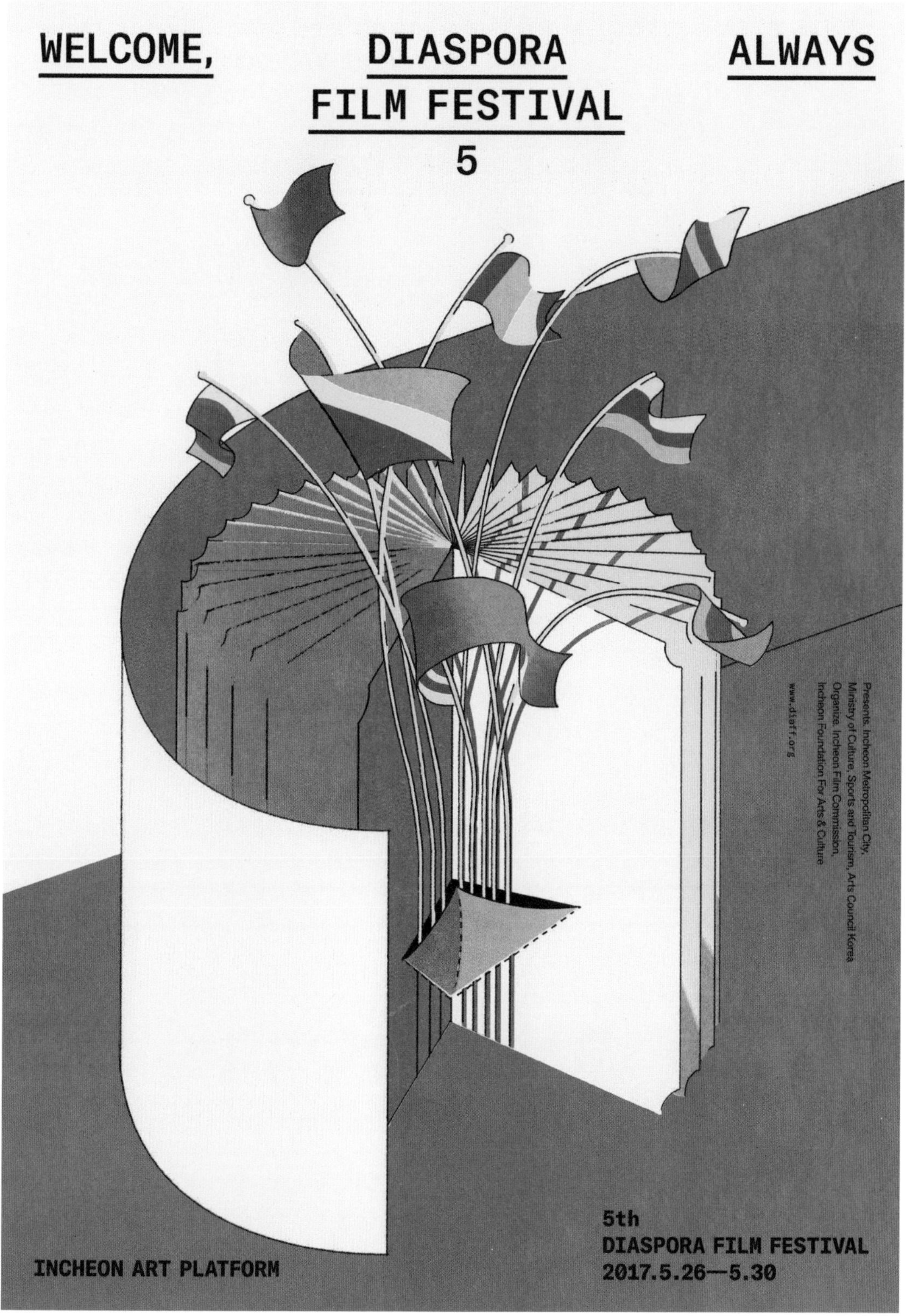

WELCOME, DIASPORA ALWAYS
FILM FESTIVAL
5

INCHEON ART PLATFORM

5th
DIASPORA FILM FESTIVAL
2017.5.26—5.30

Presents Incheon Metropolitan City,
Ministry of Culture, Sports and Tourism, Arts Council Korea
Organize Incheon Film Commission,
Incheon Foundation For Arts & Culture

www.diaff.org

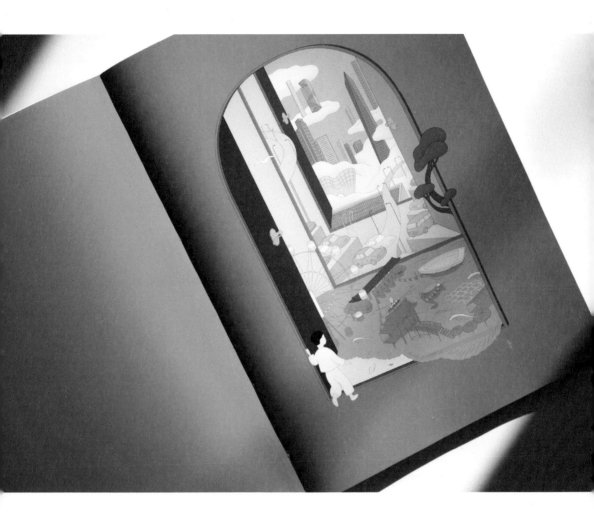

Unexpected Yeonsu

Catalogue design for the Yeonsu
Foundation For Arts & Culture
2020

→

Forum for issue 100 of Sigak

Poster for Space Beam
2019

→

Moon Prism Power

Poster design for an exhibition
2019

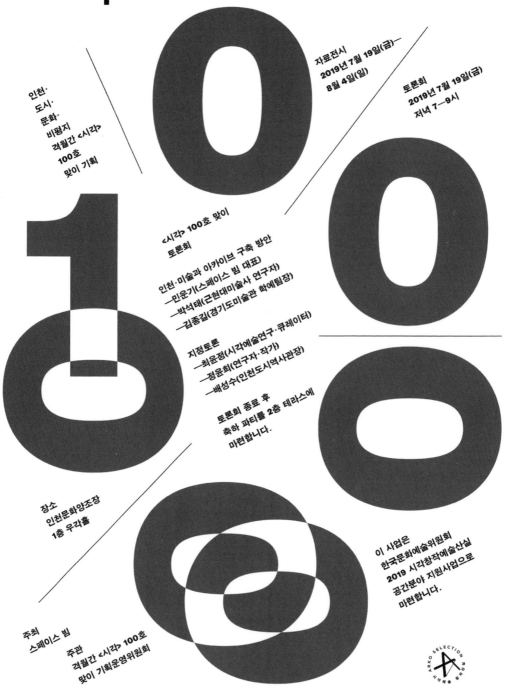

시각 1997—2019

인천·
도시·
문화·
비평지
격월간 <시각>
100호
맞이 기획

자료전시
2019년 7월 19일(금)—
8월 4일(일)

토론회
2019년 7월 19일(금)
저녁 7—9시

<시각> 100호 맞이
토론회

인천·미술과 아카이브 구축 방안
—민운기(스페이스 빔 대표)
—박석태(근현대미술사 연구자)
—김종길(경기도미술관 학예팀장)

지정토론
—최윤정(시각예술연구·큐레이터)
—정윤희(연구자·작가)
—배성수(인천도시역사관장)

토론회 종료 후
축하 파티를 2층 테라스에
마련합니다.

장소
인천문화양조장
1층 우각홀

주최
스페이스 빔

주관
격월간 <시각> 100호
맞이 기획운영위원회

이 사업은
한국문화예술위원회
2019 시각창작예술산실
공간분야 지원사업으로
마련합니다.

ARKO SELECTION

Jun
solo exhibition

moon
prism
power

2019.12.15.(sun)—2020.1.31.(fri)
Bar*Friends(7, Supyo-ro 28-gil, Jongno-gu, Seoul)
mon—sun, 7pm—2am

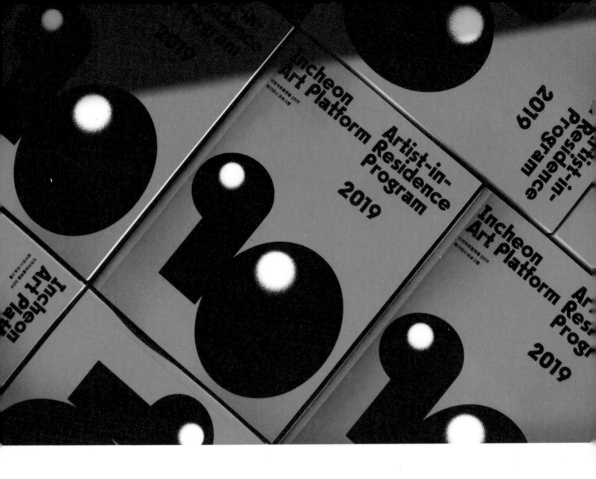

←
Tips and Tricks
Book design for curator Jinju Kim
2021

Incheon Art Platform

Residence Program

Program design for a multiplex
cultural arts center
2020

Studio Fnt studiofnt.com
Bohuy Kim kimbohuy.com
Eunjoo Hong and Hyungjae Kim hongxkim.com
Son Ayong sonayong.com
Na Kim ynkim.com
Paika paika.org
Corners Studio corners.kr
Ordinary People ordinarypeople.kr
Shin Dokho shindokho.kr
Sulki and Min sulki-min.com
BOWYER bowyer.kr
Jin & Park jinandpark.com
Triangle triangle-studio.co.kr
CFC contentformcontext.com
Everyday Practice everyday-practice.com
Hezin O ohezin.kr
DDBBMM ddbbmm.kr
Jaehoon Choi werkgraphic.com
6699press 6699press.kr